Autism

THE ULTIMATE SURVIVAL GUIDE FOR FATHERS

CHARLES J. GOWEN

Scripture taken from the King James Version of the Bible.

ISBN: 978-1-4834-5275-3 (sc)
ISBN: 978-1-4834-5276-0 (e)

Lulu Publishing Services rev. date: 06/02/2016

Contents

24 Survival Tips for Dads

Introduction

To those of you who have never been through a difficult event or a dark valley, this book might not be of any interest to you. However, I believe that most of us have experienced some degree of difficulty at some time in our lives. I would ask that you read this book and try to relate to the hurt and frustration this family felt due to a child with autism. Imagine, if you can, dealing with this illness and really not knowing what to do... Imagine, if you can, the looks and whispers of people that cut so deep. I wish I could say I knew how Jerry Gowen and his family felt. This would not be true; the truth is I didn't fully understand these families' struggles until I read the draft. This book is a wonderful testimony to faith, love, and a God given strength to help us through difficult times. Lesser men might have given up and simply left their family. Looking back on this story I felt a great deal of remorse because I simply didn't understand. Jerry has been a co-worker and friend of mine. We have talked many times about his personal struggle dealing with his son Luke. Today Luke is a different child. Today Jerry and Melina are different people. This is not to say their struggles were easy; they were not. At the end of this book I hope you will find a success story of how one family dealt with autism, and overcame their dark valley. At the end of this book I hope you will find a family that turned despair to joy at seeing their son, Luke become a child that is succeeding in life. At the end of this book I hope you look inside and strive to help someone else with their struggles of life. At the end of this book I hope you will look beyond the easy in life and try to help someone who is faced with adversity and things that are hard to understand.

Insurance Agency Manager

Bobby J. Belew

The Gowen family before autism

The Gowen family ten years later

Foreword

Beginning the process of writing this book caused me to reflect on my life in deep and meaningful ways all the way from my childhood to being the father of five wonderful children. Being the youngest of six children myself, it is nothing short of a miracle that I graduated high school given the fact that my parents had very little money and none of us had a lot of opportunity. Somehow, I made it! After several years of night and weekend classes, not to mention a wide array of jobs, my formal education was complete. It wasn't long before I was a young man with a beautiful wife, a college education, a great career, and my second son on the way. I had finally arrived at what I thought was the perfect life. Little did I know the hard times I would soon be experiencing and how challenging it was going to be to keep my family together. I never would have dreamed that these years of my "perfect life" would be the hardest ones that I have ever faced.

It is my hope and prayer that this book will encourage fathers of autistic children everywhere to keep the faith and do whatever it takes to keep their families together. Dad, I hope this book will have a positive effect on you as you read and apply the tips that worked for me to preserve my family.

The Gowen household still has its share of troubles, but I never dreamed life could be as good as it is right now!

Preface

My little ten year old boy (Luke) and his condition known as autism is the best and worst thing to ever hit my life. The last ten years have been a time of unimaginable struggle and outright suffering for Melina and me. The sad part is the struggling and suffering occurred mostly behind closed doors. Fortunately, we persevered and did not succumb to the pressures which statistics say lead a great deal of parents with special needs children to divorce. To the contrary, since Luke's diagnosis, God has blessed us with three more beautiful children, and soon Melina and I will celebrate our twentieth year of marriage. We are blessed that Luke's diagnosis has recently been changed from low functioning to high functioning! Dads, one of the purposes of this book is simply to encourage you to keep your trust in an awesome God and fight to keep your family together no matter the struggle or cost. My journey has been a long one, and my hope is that I can share with you the lessons I have learned. Just maybe, I can help lighten the load you are now bearing. Luke is truly a blessing to our family and friends, and hopefully we can be a blessing to yours. I am so excited to share our story!

The first eighteen chapters of this book will lead you step by step through the events that unfolded in our lives up through the present time. Also included are twenty-four faith based tips for daily living that I have personally used on a regular basis to keep my family together and functioning. I also encourage you to check out the ministry we have started. (godblessthelittleman.com)

Nanny paying Luke a visit

Chapter 1

LIFE BEFORE AUTISM

In February of 2005, Melina and I were on an airplane headed home from Maui. I was a Tennessee multiline insurance agent for one of the largest insurance companies in Tennessee, and we were reaping the benefits of winning a company incentive trip. Melina and I had made a lot of friends with the company and were having a great time being part of such a great organization. Our blonde haired, blue eyed, two and a half year old son Isaac was at Nana and Papa's, and we were so excited to be returning home. We had never been away from him that long, and he was the joy of our world.

The Hickman family was well on their way to completing our thirty-six hundred square foot dream home. Melina and I had purchased five-and-a-half acres from my Uncle Bill and Aunt Velma's estate sale and were super excited about getting to build our dream home on part of their property.

A year prior to becoming a Tennessee Insurance Agent, I was between jobs, so I started a tree stump grinding business. I enjoyed grinding stumps, so I kept the business and ground stumps on Saturdays for extra money. While the other agents had their outlets of hunting or playing golf, I would be out grinding stumps. Melina was finishing her accounting degree, so the extra money really helped out financially, not to mention it was a great stress reliever.

Not long after our return from Maui, we found out that Luke was on the way. I was so excited that God had sent me two boys. This meant family vacation! The insurance company had family incentive trips which were great because we got the opportunity to make friends with families all over Tennessee. These were the kind of people you wanted your kids to grow up and marry. Life was good, and everything was going great. God had truly blessed me with a great family, career, new home, side business, and large circle of friends. Melina and I were also teaching Sunday school, and our spiritual life was stronger than it had ever been. All of our hard work had truly paid off, and we were on our way to what seemed to be the perfect life. Isaac was four, and Luke was fourteen months. Isaac was born talking and was already reading. Luke could say Momma and Daddy and was a very happy baby.

Chapter 2

EARLY STAGES OF AUTISM

Melina weaned Luke and everything changed. He began, after some time, pushing his head on the floor like a bulldozer. We have home videos of Luke when he first began this, and we all thought it was funny. My Dad would call and ask what his little bulldozer was into. The next phases were no laughing matter. Melina would feed Luke baby food, and as soon as he finished eating, he would gag himself until he vomited everything he had just eaten. Within a short time, he started banging his head just as hard as he could against the hardwood floors. Before I could get to him, he already had a lump the size of a golf ball on his forehead. My Dad said it was a temper tantrum and told me to hold his head down the next time he did it, and he would stop. You guessed it. This didn't work at all. It was so awful to see such a sweet little baby boy turn into something we couldn't comprehend. His head would stay black and blue and often bleed. After months of constant diarrhea, we took Luke to a pediatrician and he diagnosed Luke with toddler diarrhea. We went back and forth to medical doctors, and they were of no help whatsoever.

We were used to being very social, but that would soon end due to Luke's wild behavior. It became increasingly difficult to go out in public and deal with all of the people constantly staring us down. Some of them were rude enough to go out of their way to tell us they never let their kids act that way. We felt helpless and did not have a clue what to do. No one in our family or circle of friends had ever experienced anything like this. It was as if someone kidnapped my son and left me with a breathing shell of a boy with no emotion or identity.

Word of Advice

To all you fathers who are in the early stages of dealing with autism, hang in there and don't give up hope! With the right therapies and diet, your child has a great chance of making significant improvement. Also, remember it is your child that is locked up in there and he or she cannot help it at this stage. By all means, don't give up, and don't let the rest of your family fall by the wayside.

Chapter 3

STRIVING TO BE NORMAL

Prayer became more of a reality to me during this time than ever before. For the first time in my life, I could not out work my problems. It seemed as if no one could help us. We felt like most of our family and friends were avoiding us and didn't want us around. It was like we had leprosy. I somehow kept it together and continued to win incentive trips with the company. We had to pass on the big trips like the Alaskan Cruise, but we continued going on the family trips. Luke was like a walking time bomb because it was anybody's guess when he was going to explode, but you could bet that everyone within screaming distance would stare us down. We would go out as a family of four to a restaurant, and I would go in by myself. I would get a table and order my food first. Next, I would inform the waiter that we had a special needs child that might get unruly. Afterwards, I would bring the rest of the family in and scarf my food down as quickly as possible. More times than not, I would end up grabbing Luke up and making a run for the door while people of all kinds would give me "the look". Once in the car, I would put on my work tunes (ear muffs) to drown out the constant screaming and wait on Melina and Isaac to finish their peaceful meal together.

One day a very rude woman actually yelled at Luke in a restaurant. Melina tried to explain that something was wrong with him, and she told Melina to keep him at home. This was the closest I had ever come to punching a female in the face. Thankfully, my Christian upbringing saved me from doing something that I would later regret, but I did tell her I would hit her if she opened her big mouth again! I quickly rushed my family out of the restaurant with my wife in tears. I returned to pay for our drinks because the food had not been brought out yet. To my dismay, everyone was standing and clapping their hands while an older gentleman was giving the rude woman a good old fashion cussing. The manager gave me the food to go and refused payment.

Chapter 4

FIRST AND SECOND DIAGNOSIS

Determined to find out what was wrong with our child, we took the advice of a friend and took Luke to a specialist. Once we were at the appointment, Luke was in rare form. He was running around the office and screaming to the top of his lungs. The doctor was not very kid friendly, and she was real quick to tell us that Luke was without a doubt autistic. There is no doubt that the doctor was very competent, but she came off extremely rude and offended us. In her defense, we were so beaten down that it didn't take much to offend us. Melina was convinced that something would heal our son and would not in any way accept this first diagnosis. From this point on, she would stay up almost all night every night researching every natural cure and treatment she could find. Melina put college on the back burner, and the once fun business of grinding tree stumps became a way of paying for special diets, doctor appointments, and treatments for Luke.

The tension was so thick around our home it could be cut with a knife. Up until this time, Melina and I had never had a real fight much less any real marital problems. Putting a fake smile on to sell insurance became harder and harder as the days went by. Luke's first diagnosis was at three and the second was at four years old. As tough as it was at the time, we accepted the second one. We simply lived in denial hoping that Luke would somehow get better from fourteen months to age four.

As a father, it was very difficult to have all the dreams of raising two boys and watching them play together as normal brothers and not getting to see that come about. Quite simply, my heart was completely broken. Luke said Momma and Daddy at fourteen months and didn't say it again until he was four years old. Melina would not even attempt a restaurant for the next three years. We would eat at home or occasionally go to a drive-through. After a woman asked us during one of Luke's public meltdowns if he would have been the first child would we have had any more children, Melina stopped going to Isaac's baseball games.

People at church did not understand or help in any way, so we would rotate Sundays. We gave up our Sunday school classes, and we would rotate staying home with Luke. After five long years of not sitting on a pew together as a family, and no spiritual growth, we decided to visit a much larger church. Some of our close friends invited us to their church, and we took them up on it. The preaching was awesome, and the people were nice. The nursery was top of the line and it was a breath of fresh air from what we were accustomed to. On the third visit I had full plans of joining until I saw my wife coming out of the nursery with tears in her eyes. Someone had left a very mean note on the door inside the nursery for my wife concerning Luke's behavior. The church we visited those three weeks was a great church full of great people. They just weren't prepared and equipped to deal with an autistic child. This is one of the reasons I am so passionate about autism awareness. It's crucial that people in our society are aware of what autism is and how to deal with it. Had these church workers been equipped with the knowledge of how to deal with an autistic child, I am convinced everyone's experience would have been very positive and productive.

Chapter 5

GAME FACE AND RELOCATION

After living in denial for four years and having all our joy ripped out from under us, Melina and I put our game faces on. She poured every bit of energy she could into research. If there was a diet, therapy, or related story about autism on the internet, she read about it. Her main focus was on Luke's condition and well- being. Our cabinets were full of all kinds of different vitamins, oils, and special foods.

My game face was quite different from hers because I was and still am the sole bread-winner of our family. I knew that I had to toughen my skin and pull up my boot straps if we were going to survive this costly situation that had been thrown at us. It was also obvious that the new home I enjoyed so much was in no way safe for Luke. It had hardwood and tile floors upstairs and concrete in the garage and basement. It also had a spiral staircase, a twenty foot deck, and fourteen foot retainer walls. With Luke's head banging and wild behavior, it was not a safe place for him to live. Moreover, with the much added expense that autism brought to my family, it was obvious that we desperately needed to downsize our home. After many late night talks and budget meetings, we made the decision to put our dream home on the market. It sold in less than a month.

We found an older ranch- style brick on seven-and-a-half acres and closed on it the same day as the sale of our new home. Needless to say, it was in need of many repairs. It had an old school bus in the back yard full of junk, an old car with a tree growing through the hood where the engine used to be, several old buildings, and an old two story house that I eventually tore down. It also had an old pond that barely held any water. I eventually filled it in because of the fear of one of my boys drowning. The roof of our new house was bad, and we had to completely redo the inside. The central unit went out during the first month I owned it. We had forty-five days to get out of our new dream house, so I worked every weekend and every night. I would get two or three hours of sleep, put my fake smile on, and head into the office. It was so depressing to move out of a new home on family land that I was so proud of to a dump. We have now lived in our not so dream house for eight years. After several remodels and a ton of money spent, it has worked out great for us. The move helped us financially at the time and the new neighbors who are mostly older people have all but adopted my family and its challenging situations.

We have truly learned what it is like to live one day at a time out of pure survival mode. Luke's expenses were enormous. I spent eight hundred dollars per month out of my own pocket for years for a professional to come to our house to work with Luke. Melina made an appointment with an autism clinic after they told us it would be covered on our health insurance policy. I took a day off work and drove two hours for a one hour appointment. The so-called professionals did not run many tests and only asked me questions like what color was my great grandmother's eyes. The clinic sent us a bill for seven thousand dollars that ended up not being covered on my insurance policy. I fought with them for a year before they turned it over to a collection agency. In an effort to protect my credit, I called them to make a deal. I told them I had twenty- five hundred dollars and they could take it or leave it. They refused at first, but when I threatened to take my story to their local news channel they immediately sent an updated bill for the amount of twenty-five hundred dollars. We also made a trip to Hot Springs Arkansas to a natural doctor that turned out to be another disappointment in our quest to help our son. We tried everything we could think of to find help for Luke. Some things worked, but most things didn't. During these years, I pushed Melina to finish her college degree. She didn't lack very many classes, and I knew it would be good for her to get her mind off autism. Even though I knew I would have to bear down in order to cover the added expense of tuition, it really was a great move for us.

Word of Advice

Dads, the one thing I can tell you is to try something different to survive. Depending on your specific situation, you may need to sell your house, cars, change careers, start a business, or relocate. I found myself doing all of the above to keep it together. The constant screaming, along with the enormous financial pressure, will consume you! Seek as much help for your child as possible and be creative in the monetary arena.

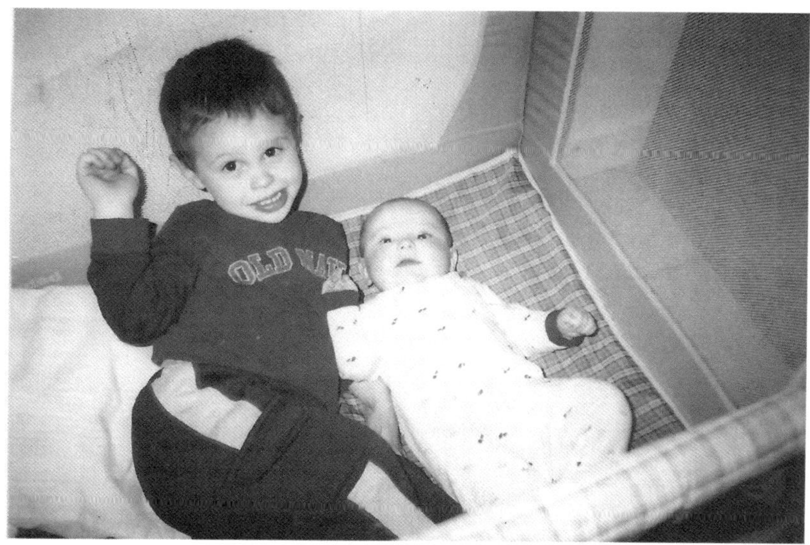

Luke and Leah

Chapter 6

LEAH

On November 30, 2008 our third child Leah Jane Gowen arrived. Our family and circle of friends thought we were crazy for adding another child into our mix. In my research, I found that autistic children do a lot better when they have siblings, so we left it up to God to send us more children and prayed that they would be healthy. Also, I didn't want our oldest son Isaac to grow up without any normal siblings and no help for Luke as we got older. Melina took her last test the week after Leah was born. I was so proud of her. She earned a Bachelor of Accounting degree with a 3.9 GPA while raising an autistic child and carrying our baby girl. Moreover, she was taking great care of me and Isaac. I actually have a picture of Melina holding Leah at her graduation in her cap and gown. What a surprise God had for us. Leah's birth would turn out to be the first sign of emotion Luke showed. No matter where Luke was when he heard Leah crying, he would run to pet her. This, coming from a child that had never hugged me or his mother and could only say one or two words, was a complete shock.

Luke was extremely low functioning, and I had seen enough videos of teen aged autistic kids to know what was coming our way. During this time Luke had started early intervention provided by the State of Tennessee. We were blessed with a lady by the name of Miss Beth that taught Luke how to talk. She had a special way of getting the most out of Luke. It seemed like Leah grew up overnight. She taught Luke more than all the therapies combined. It was like God sent her to rescue

Luke from himself. She is very tough, and I joke to my boys that Leah is everything I always wanted in a son.

With Luke's regular meltdowns and the addition of another child, the pressure grew more and more. At the office, I made a huge sale. (The largest that had ever come through our office at the time.) One of my clients invested a lot of money into a life insurance policy and it qualified me for every incentive trip that year with enough left over to send the whole office to Disney World. This would be our last family trip. If you can, imagine a sixteen hour drive with a seven year old and a four year old autistic boy that screamed round trip. Plus, he screamed the whole time we were at Disney World while we were pushing Leah in a stroller. Get that picture in your mind and you will understand why this was our last trip. To top it off, I forgot to mention that I took the in-laws. It was, by far, one of the most miserable weeks of my life that I can recall. It was so hard watching all the normal families getting to enjoy their children while we struggled just to survive. Melina's joy, as well as mine, was nowhere to be found in Leah's early years. Sadly, the only smile that existed on our face was the "fake it until you make it" kind.

Word of Advice

Dads, more children definitely helped Luke. If you don't want any more or can't have any more kids, I would strongly recommend adopting or at least keeping your child as socially active as possible. The last thing you want to do is isolate your autistic child. As hard as it may be at the time, the best thing you can do is keep pushing hard to stay in the public and stay involved socially.

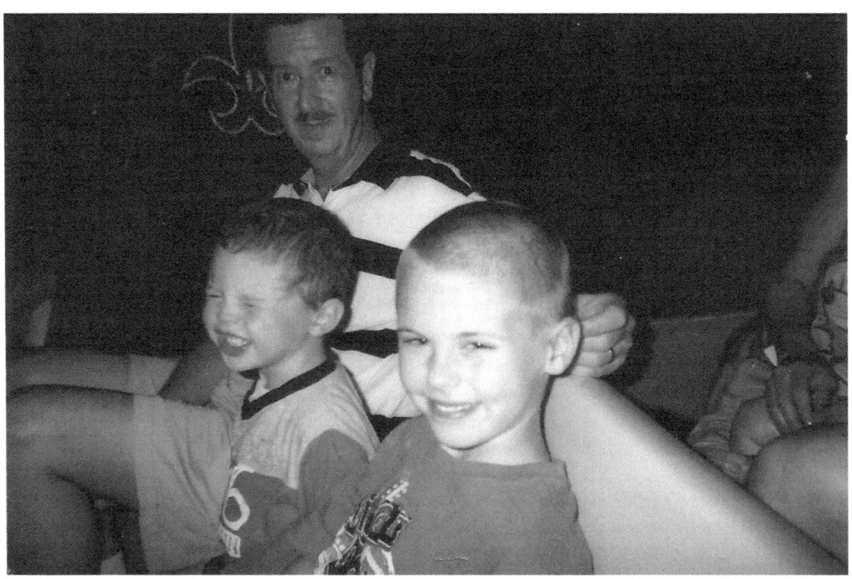

Disney World (Isaac, Luke, and Papa Bailey)

Chapter 7

DIVINE APPOINTMENT

Luke was almost five years old and for the past two years I had not performed very well on my job. My production was up and down like a yo-yo and my joy was a thing of the past. Until this time, my high on life and outgoing personality had played a key part in my success, but I was so beaten down spiritually, mentally, and physically that I simply could not fake it any longer. I would cut trees and grind stumps on Saturdays and afternoons to keep our bills paid and avoid financial ruin. It felt great to work outside, but when I would return to the office I would suffocate. With a broken spirit, it was a monumental challenge to sell insurance while looking at photos on the wall of my once happy family. Operating equipment and running a chain saw permitted me to work out some of the hurt and provided a release that couldn't be found sitting behind a desk. I would take long lunches to let Melina take a nap during the day.

Dealing with Luke and the other children plus all the late night research for treatments and cures left Melina exhausted most of the time. She was convinced that something or someone was out there that could help Luke. It was during this time something very interesting happened. I was cutting trees in Franklin on Labor Day (the office was closed) and noticed a man standing in the road watching me as I worked. I just assumed that he was in need of my service, so I gave him one of my cards. Little did I know that he owned the largest tree company in the area, and I actually needed his service. After talking for a while, the subject of Luke's condition came up, and he strongly recommended that we take him to his wife's doctor. He said that Dr. Kalb was a natural doctor and his treatments had really helped his wife's rare condition. Desperate to try anything, Melina made the appointment with Dr. Kalb. That was seven years ago, and we still use him on a regular basis. Needless to say, the tree man from Franklin and I are close friends to this day. After seeing Dr. Kalb it was only a matter of months before a lot of the toxins were gone from Luke's system. He no longer had diarrhea and the dark circles under his eyes were gone. It was a divine appointment that day when I met my good friend J.D Myers. It was the appointment that led to Luke's improvements.

Word of Advice

Dads, don't take autism personally! Trust me, someone or something will offend you every day if you look at your situation negatively! Life is always full of changes, and having an autistic child will definitely alter the life style that you are accustomed to. With that in mind, stay calm and look at your situation as a blessing from God. Autistic children are very different. They have an innocence about them that is priceless. Melina and I have found that the majority of the public are uneducated about autism. That being said, most people would go out of their way to help you if they understood. One time I made the mistake of asking a lady when her baby was due, and come to find out she was not even expecting. Needless to say, I won't ask that question now under any circumstances, so go easy on the unknowing public.

Chapter 8

MAJOR CAREER MOVE

At the office, my regional manager knew I was having a hard time with my family situation, and he was very patient with me. The past year had been an absolute fight for survival to maintain job performance. In recent years, I had been the regional manager of a large contracting company and was given the credit for running the best operation within several states. For the first time in my life, I found myself in a place where I was doing a terrible job and it was very obvious that my office manager was not pleased with me. How could he be? I wasn't getting the job done!

After much prayer and many late night talks with Melina, I made the decision to resign my job in order to save face. I set up a meeting with my regional manager and gave him the thirty day notice which was required in our contract. He completely understood and told me he would definitely consider letting me come back in the future since I was leaving on such good terms.

I've always been a hard worker with a strong work ethic, but I was not in the shape spiritually, mentally, or physically to keep selling insurance. With only a couple days of tree work lined up, a tractor, a stump grinder, and a dump trailer, I parted ways with the company I was once so proud to be a part of. My regional manager showed me a great deal of respect and generously paid me through December.

I've actually been blessed over the past five years to do a great deal of work for my former customers and co- workers. Most of them told me they miss me at the office and that they always enjoyed doing business with me. In fact, I have a great relationship with the folks in Lawrence County. They trust me and still call me on a regular basis for advice on their insurance. I'm also grateful that God has allowed me the opportunity to restore some work relationships that were very strained at the time of my departure on the local level.

Most people didn't understand our situation, and I wrongly assumed that they did. All the agents are great people and. more importantly, friends. I am so glad that I am getting to help people understand autism and its effects on people's personal and professional lives. It is really important to educate people so that they understand and have a working knowledge of autism so they can help with this diagnosis. I am convinced that if people just have the facts, they are more than willing to lend a helping hand no matter the circumstances.

Word of Advice

Dads, we must promote autism awareness! It is my hope that by sharing my personal experience you will be allowed to have victory over your situation. Personally, autism has changed the way I look at people because it's difficult to know exactly what a man is going through. I've learned that things aren't always as they seem. That's why I want to encourage you to be unafraid to tell your story as well.

Chapter 9

ELI

It was literally two weeks after I left the company that Melina sprang the news on me that number four was on the way. I had just quit a professional career to run my own business cutting trees and grinding stumps and here comes more stress. I was worried how I was going to provide and where the work was going to come from.

Four tornadoes hit Lawrence County the following spring, and we worked daylight to dark most of the year. I was terrified of heights and had always hired out the bucket work on my jobs, but with the tornado damage so severe no one had time to work for me. There were trees down everywhere and my phone was blowing up. You guessed it dads! I did what any hard headed hillbilly with a Bachelors Degree in Business, a class A CDL license, and an insurance license would do. I bought a thirty-seven foot bucket truck and forced myself to get over the fear of heights. At the end of the each day, I couldn't tell if I was worn out from work or fear. After running the thirty-seven foot bucket for about four months, I soon found out it wasn't enough truck and I stepped up to a sixty foot truck. I can't begin to describe how busy we were.

I had to sell my company stock to make it through the first winter, but by the end of the year we were doing well. This all sounds great, but during my first year of business I would be so worn out by the weekend that I was of no use to my family and very difficult to be around. I was thick skinned, bitter, and determined to succeed.

On June 11, 2011, Eli Joseph Gowen arrived. I had taken a week off with my first three children but not with Eli. When Eli arrived and I was sure that everything was good with Momma at the hospital, I left and cut trees. God really sent us a blessing with Eli. He is, to this day, the sweetest and most generous child we have. If I take him to a store, he insists that I buy something for the rest of the kids. With the arrival of Eli, my wife's beautiful smile along with her joy reappeared after five long years.

Word of Advice

Dads, if you are struggling right now to keep it together make sure to try something different. While the dramatic changes that fit my family may or may not fit your situation, I'm convinced that a change of pace will help you. For example, keep the job you have because good jobs are hard to come by. Start a small side business. You would be amazed what an extra thousand dollars a month will do for your family! Furthermore, you can easily make that much money pressure washing houses and concrete on Saturday mornings and still have time to hang out with the family in the afternoon. If you can find something that you enjoy doing, (woodwork, handy man stuff, etc.) you not only have something that helps financially but also something to look forward to.

Chapter 10

NOAH

On October 10, 2014, Noah Paul Gowen arrived. You guessed it; baby number five was here! I found out that I was going to have baby number five as my fortieth birthday was soon approaching and I was two hundred and fourteen pounds. I was physically worn out from years of running wide open. Determined to get ready for having a baby in my forties, I got on a strict diet, lost thirty five pounds, and ran a 5K fundraiser with a friend. My mother- in-law told me that it was nearly impossible to lose weight after forty and in eight weeks I proved her wrong through motivation and pride.

When Noah arrived, I had owned and operated a full tree service for five years and was making more money than I had ever made in my life. I had the best tree equipment around and was leaps and bounds ahead of my competitors in every measurable category. To the detriment of the whole family, I had hidden myself into my business like a drug addict. I ate, breathed and slept the tree business. With the cutting edge equipment and the best help in the business, my right hand man and I could do the work of a five man crew in a day. I had just purchased a new top of the line articulating loader, and it was no doubt that Affordable Tree Removal and Stump Grinding was the best of the best. From the outside I'm sure everything looked great, but on the inside….the inside was anything but great. To make things worse, the day before Noah was born I was thrown from a loader and tore my right rotator cuff. On top of it all, it rained so much the next three months that we barely got to work. The combined stress of family and running a business had completely sucked all the life out of me. The seven years of dealing with an autistic child and all the difficulties that are entailed with that had beaten Melina and me down.

The thought of adding another child was more than I could bear at the time, not to mention the fact that I had seven years of bitterness and heartache swelling up inside me. The pain medicine for my shoulder didn't help matters any because it ended up being a narcotic. It jacked me up to the point that I would go several days in a row with no sleep. I had truly learned how to suck it up and push forward in life despite both my circumstances and how I truly felt. I had left the insurance company with no gray hair and now it was salt and pepper. I could not raise my right shoulder above my head, and my family was falling apart. The tree business no longer gave me any satisfaction. I was bitter at God, my family, my former office manager, people that made rude comments, and pretty much everything else in life.

Me and John

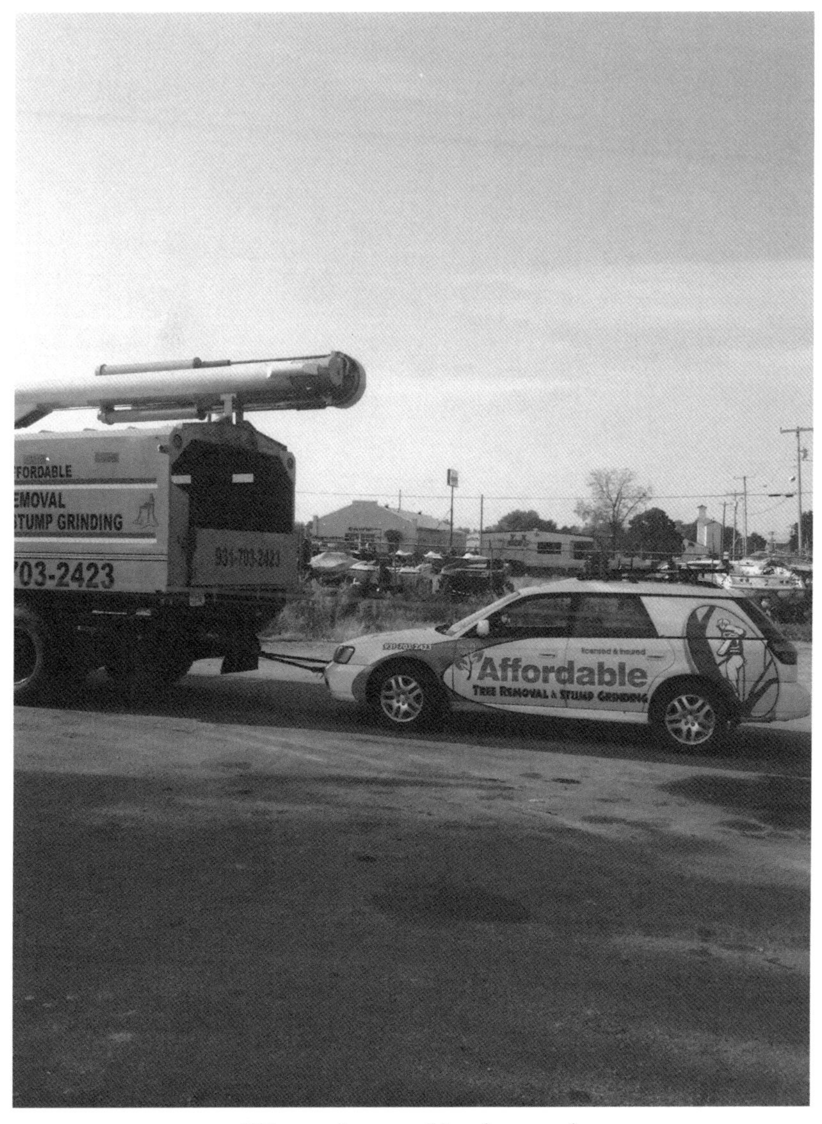

Wrapped car and bucket truck

Papa Jim Gowen "Pretty Jim"

Word of Advice

Dads, most of us men have enough pride to push forward in life and get things accomplished in our own strength. This is a good thing and a bad thing. If you are not careful, you will become so hard that it is nearly impossible to be the husband and father God intended you to be. God gave us a provider instinct and intended for us to use it. Put God first, and then apply the tough, manly, daddy stuff. Then you will have the right heart for your family!

Chapter 11

GOD'S ATTENTION GETTERS

As a teenager I partied a lot and got in trouble with the law from time to time. I actually outran several police cars one night and was out celebrating my victory and laughing about it only to return and find a note on my truck from my dad that the police had a warrant out for him. You guessed right. My truck was registered in my dad's name. Needless to say, this one didn't go over very well at all.

After high school graduation, I started trade school knowing this was probably the best I could do in life. I was half-way through my first quarter and got a full time job at a factory working eight to twelve hour shifts. After a month of full time school, full time factory work, and part time partying, I woke up in a Nashville hospital. I soon learned from my family that I had fallen asleep at the wheel, flipped my truck eight times, and was ejected from my truck. There was little to no chance of surviving a horrific wreck like that, but I escaped with my life and a DUI charge. This was a game changer for me at the early age of eighteen. God spared my life, and now He had my attention. I enrolled in college part time and continued to work the factory job. A year later, I enrolled full time and took on a part time job to pay for tuition. I left the party scene and all my so called friends, got active in church, and set out to make a better life for myself.

After Noah was born, we had a couple of close calls in the tree business. I know now that God was once again trying to get my attention. That year Melina gave me a new journal for Christmas and on January 1, 2015, I found myself writing in it in my most miserable condition.

Lord, please help me to help myself
Lord, please help me to have the desire to help myself
Lord, please restore unto me the joy of my salvation
I haven't pleased you in a long time

I was what I refer to as a successful failure. I had filled the void of a broken heart and a challenging situation with a business and worldly things. I had failed to be the spiritual leader of my home, and my wife was living like a single mother of five. I had done everything in my own power to get the bitterness off, but my heart was so hard nothing seemed to work. By February, God answered my prayer. I was up late one night and stumbled across a Christian comedian. At the end of his routine, he said we were all like a house and Jesus wants to come into our house. Then he went on to say that we were ok with having him outside the door where we could call on him when we needed him. We were ok with him being in the front room that we keep clean, but he wants to live in the entire house. He then went on to say that some of us used to let him live in the entire house, but something had moved him out. The latter part of that message fit me and knocked my legs out from under me. I had completely used work as my drug for years, and I was so miserable and full of bitterness. There was no joy in spending good quality time with my family. I couldn't even enjoy the simplest day to day blessings. At three O'clock in the A.M. with Melina and the kids asleep, God had truly answered my prayer. The tough game face, fake it until you make it, got something to prove, not going to back down tough guy stuff was officially over!

November 14, 1992 near death truck crash

Close call in the bucket

Word of Advice

I have always had a gift of helping others with their problems and this also became a way of coping with my own struggles in life. I was like the mechanic that fixes everyone else's car and drives a piece of junk. Don't put the needs of others ahead of your family. Dads, try to deal with the tough issues one at a time with autism or it will pile up on you. Be honest with yourself and by all means try to handle problems with a clear mind or you will make a jumpy move that you will regret. Nevertheless, trust God and depend on him to help you deal with the pressing issues of life. You don't have anything to prove and you simply can't do it all on your own.

Chapter 12

SURRENDERING TO GOD'S WILL

We are blessed to be a part of a small country church full of down to earth people who love on Luke and the rest of my family. Despite our challenging situations, they don't look down on us or make us feel unwelcome. The church has learned what I've learned. Raising Luke has taught me how God loves. It's simple; He loves like Luke loves. Luke doesn't care how much money you have, how many times you have been divorced, what nationality you are, or what your outward appearance happens to be. Luke looks at your heart. If you are receptive of him, he will pile up with you. In fact, if you show him a small amount of attention, he will ask you if he can go home with you. Having Luke taught us what it is like to be the least of these.

It truly humbled and amazed me to see which people showed up to love on my family in the hard times. I could tell you story after story of all the hurtful encounters my wife and I have experienced, but that is not the purpose of this book. God has delivered me from that hurt. Believe it or not, in one night, God allowed me to get all the bitterness out of my system. After getting all that bitterness out of my system, I had more joy than ever before and I felt like a twenty year old man. It was like God gave me a double scoop of the joy I had once known several years ago. He showed me a vivid picture of what I had become and where I was failing as a husband and father. Immediately, several people came to mind that I had hard feeling toward. I believe God laid them on my heart. Being a hyper get it done kind of person, I couldn't get to people fast enough to ask their forgiveness for all the past bitter feelings I had toward them.

My family and circle of friends, for the most part, thought I was having a mid-life crisis or that I had lost my mind. It absolutely flipped people out to see me so high on life and full of joy, and their assumptions were far from the truth. It also hit me that my former officer manager would never have treated me the way he did during my last couple of years with the company had he truly understood what we were going through at the time or had a better understanding of autism. I'm sure he just thought I loved the tree business better than selling insurance which would have been my evaluation too if I were in his position. I called him and we had a great conversation. I apologized for my poor job performance and years of past bitterness, and he told me that he did not have a clue about the degree of my family's past hardship with Luke. I have a lot of respect for him, and we currently have a great relationship. After surrendering to God's will for my life, my wife looked prettier, I had a new found love for life, and I looked at my large family as a blessing instead of hardship. My whole world became brighter, and God gave me a peace beyond worldly understanding.

Word of Advice

Dads, if you have never trusted Jesus Christ as your savior now is the time to do so. Furthermore, if you have trusted Him but you are depending on yourself or worldly things, surrender your all to Him and let Him carry all your burdens as you live each day. I made the mistake of putting work and other people's problems ahead of my family. Work in moderation and help people the way that fits you. Never let other people's problems come between you and your family. Put God first, your immediate family second, and everything else where it fits.

Chapter 13

EFFECTS OF AUTISM ON THE FAMILY

I am now forty one years old, Melina is thirty nine, Isaac is thirteen, Luke is ten, Leah is seven, Eli is four, and Noah is sixteen months. I have put a full five years into the tree business and half of my hair has turned gray. I have a chainsaw scar on my right hand, a large one across my stomach, and I will soon undergo a corrective surgery on my right shoulder to repair the rotator cuff. It has been a year since God restored my joy, and I've made several strides at improving my family life.

As I mentioned earlier, I am a firm believer in doing something different and one of my favorite quotes is from Albert Einstein. "The definition of insanity is doing the same thing over and over again and expecting different results." Once again, I have found myself putting on the game face except this time I put God first to the best of my abilities. The first step was getting back in the word of God. Next, I restructured the business by downsizing. I sold several pieces of equipment and my equipment lot. I also gave a couple of things away. I consulted with my accountant, and due to my high tax bracket, we determined that I would come out better on my taxes if I donated a couple of things. I moved my equipment back home where I first started the small business that I once so enjoyed. Bigger is not always better, and it is better to have less of the world and be close with God and family. I remember a preacher saying one time that if you had too much to serve God, you had better get rid of some of it. This didn't make much sense to me at the time, but it became a reality to me at age forty. I also began to strive every day to put God first, family second, and let the rest fall where it may.

My family and friends once again thought I had gone off the deep end. The rumor was started that I was giving my business away and that I was not going to be able to provide for my family. It spread like wildfire. Actually, the truth was the very opposite. By downsizing and cutting down on overhead, I could work half as much and clear the same money which allowed me to spend more time with my family and be a better husband and father. Everyone was so used to me being a workaholic that it flipped them out to see me slow down and enjoy all the blessings of life that I had been running past in my pursuit of success. The one big thing that I did wrong was to spoil my other children to make up for the hardships that Luke's condition brought to our family. I chased money and over worked myself when all they wanted was my time. With God's help, we have been slowly changing the path of our parenting by focusing on spiritual leadership and spending quality time as a family. We know that we didn't get in this shape overnight, and no doubt, it will take time to turn the ship in the right direction.

My oldest son Isaac has adapted well. He is a straight A student and a great athlete. He is a grown man inside a five foot one inch body. He will most likely become a preacher or a lawyer. He has a very discerning sprit and cannot stand for someone to be dishonest. It's simple with Isaac; right is right and wrong is wrong. Also, Isaac is a big help with the baby as well as the rest of the children. He is a real blessing, and it is an honor to be his father. Leah has paid the price for being directly under Luke. She is a sweet little girl, but we were so exhausted dealing with Luke that she picked up a lot of rebellious behavior. With God's help, we pray that she will continue to improve. Eli has also been affected by both Luke and Leah's behavior, but he is coming right along. Noah is just a baby, and since we know what not to do with him, we are hoping he dodges the behavior bullet.

Word of Advice

Dads, you must look at your family as a team and play together. To take it a step further, it is more like an Army platoon, and you must teach your family to fight through difficult times together. Have family meetings, pray together, and by all means get everyone's input on the pressing issues of life. Use these hard times to draw closer to your wife instead of allowing them to push you apart. Another big help is to find at least one good friend or pastor with a listening ear. Remember, your wife is in this with you, and she already has her plate full.

Chapter 14

LAUGHING MISERABLY

I have always enjoyed making people laugh. As I mentioned earlier, I am the youngest of six children, and we were poor as far as worldly things go. My parents had a hard time making ends meet, but the one thing I learned from them was to always find something to laugh about. We worked hard and laughed a lot as a family.

My dad worked out of town, and my mom stayed busy raising big gardens and tending to all of us kids. Other than our station wagon and three TV channels, we were like Amish as far as modern amenities go. I tell people all the time that I invented Capri pants in grade school because I often wore high water hand me downs. In fact, I still growl as I eat in fear that someone will try to take my food away from me.

I can still make Melina laugh like a school girl after all these years, but during the hard times it was a challenge to get even a chuckle out of her. I remember one morning she was up making coffee with tears in her eyes, and I slipped a set of bubba teeth in and began to serenade her with an old Alabama classic.

Sometimes her morning coffee's way too strong, and sometimes what she says she says all wrong, But right or wrong she's there beside me like only a friend would be, and that's close enough to perfect for me.
Alabama. "Close Enough To Perfect For Me."
Mountain Music. RCA,
1982.

This one floored her, and it was a much needed laugh for the both of us. She has always loved New York, and sometimes I would pretend she actually lived there. I would go on to thank her for being so nice to my kids and treating them like they were hers. I would always end it with "what time does your flight leave?" This one worked great at relieving the stress temporarily.

The Bible says, "a merry heart doeth good like medicine," and it is so true. Laughter is without a doubt the best medicine. Not only did I hide in work, I hid in making people laugh as well. Our God given strengths will become our weaknesses if we don't put Him first in our daily walk. While others would be laughing at my unique sense of humor, I would be hurting on the inside. I was like a cheap gold plated watch. Everything looked good on the outside, but I was completely miserable on the inside before God healed my broken condition.

We are doing better by leaps and bounds and I work a steady schedule for the most part unless a storm blows through. I must admit I almost feel retired after giving up the wide open chase. At first, it was a hard adjustment, but it was the best move I ever made.

Word of Advice

Dads, having more children helped Luke more than anything. It is a joy to spend good quality time with all of my children. Early on, I didn't keep the right balance with my children. I caught myself spending more time with Luke thinking it was giving the rest of the family a break. You must be determined to have quality time with the entire family. It is a lot of work and very challenging, but it is well worth the efforts to push forward. Don't let autism label your family or keep you from living a productive life.

Chapter 15

LUKE'S PROGRESS AND SPECIAL GIFTS

This chapter is my favorite by far to write. With the right diets and treatments and the awesome people God put in our life to help us, Luke is now in the third grade as a regular student. He is at the top of his class in several areas. His teachers refer to him as Mr. Webster because he can spell better than most of his class. Also, his communication skills are exceptional, and he never meets a stranger. He has really come out of his shell in the past couple of years. It's hard to believe that he just jumps right out of the vehicle and walks to class by himself. In the early years of school, he literally had holes kicked in the dash of my car. I had to take the kids to school every morning because Melina was not strong enough to force Luke out. Also, we were blessed with a great public school that did all they could to help us with Luke and push him to the next level. He is very social, has a great personality and vocabulary, and has a real sense of humor. Luke still has his meltdowns, but it is nothing like before. I can usually get him calmed down in a short matter of time. I can make funny faces at him and undergo a strong round of tickling and within minutes he is back on the level. Everyone loves "The Luke" and all the teachers refer to my other children as Luke's brothers or Luke's sister like he is some kind of royalty.

I am amazed at the things Luke is interested in. We took the training wheels off of Leah's bicycle last summer, and she was so excited that she could ride a few feet without wrecking that she ran in the house to tell her mother. Luke, on the other hand, had never ridden a bicycle, but he had spent hours studying it. He got on it and rode it down our long driveway and back without wrecking. He parked it like a pro and said "I like bicycles." I was completely blown away at this one.

Some of our best laughs come from Luke because he takes everything so literally. Here are some examples.

Our preacher picked him up one Sunday after church and said "Boy you sure are heavy; you must have a belly full of rocks." Luke asked us every day for the next six months if he had swallowed a rock.

One time, Luke and I were at a friend's hardware store and Tony, the owner, lit a cigarette. Luke asked him what that was. Tony replied," It's a stink weed." Luke asked him if it was for big people, and Tony replied, "It's for dumb people." Luke then went on to tell Tony that Isaac could use some of them because "he's dumb at him all the time."

He asked a long haired man at a store in Florence Alabama if he was a girl.

My dad scolded Luke for trying to go up in the sound booth at his church. At that time, Luke had never called him by his name. When we got home Luke said "I don't like Jim Gowen."

He asked a somewhat overweight friend of mine if he had a baby in his belly.

My cousin Fred asked Luke, "Where did you get that haircut at?" and Luke replied, "On my head".

He would torture his cat by over petting it and squeezing it until it sounded like it was dying. The funny thing was that the cat must have gotten addicted to the abuse. It would go out of its way to find Luke to undergo more "therapy". One time, I heard a very different noise. It was tat, tat, tat, and meow. Luke had the cover off of a fan and was using the cat's back feet to stop the fan from turning. Needless to say, we had to get rid of the fan.

As you can see, Luke is a very funny character. He either likes you or doesn't like you. If I go into most of the small businesses in Lawrence County by myself they want to know where Luke is. Everyone loves "The Luke". Even people that look like they have never smiled a day in their lives light up when he starts the interrogation process on them.

What's your name? How old are you? What road do you live on? How many pounds are you? This last one has put me in some embarrassing situations. Luke loves to look at maps and play on my GPS. He can tell you most of the roads in Lawrence County. Also, he knows every town between Florence, Alabama and Nashville, Tennessee in order. He also knows every state. He is truly a joy and keeps our life interesting because you never know what he is going to say or do.

I'm thankful that I didn't give up years ago and miss all the blessings and benefits that we are reaping today. The biggest blessing is that we ate our first meal as a family of seven last year without anyone staring us down or making us feel unwelcome.

Word of Advice

Life is not over dads. By all means, don't play the victim card or give up on your marriage. You don't have a bad situation; you have a different one. Be yourself and deal with life one day at a time. Wake up early, hold your head up, lift a few weights and face the day with the courage of a warrior.

Chapter 16

WHAT CAUSES AUTISM?

Dads, I'm not a doctor. I don't even play one on TV, so I'm not about to get into the argument of vaccinations. In my opinion, Luke had a weak immune system, and the medical staff gave him too many shots at one time. His system simply could not handle it. It took years to get all the metals out of Luke's system. We actually sent his stool sample to France several times and purchased thousands of dollars of special food, and dietary supplements. We paid a small fortune to doctors, and we really don't have a clue what actually causes autism.

To be truthful, the cause is irrelevant once your child is diagnosed. I do know for a fact that had we not taken Luke to a natural doctor, he would not be in the third grade as a normal student today. I hope and pray that the medical field finds out soon what causes this detrimental childhood developmental disorder.

In my common sense way of thinking, it seems to me that some tests should be administered on a child before the immunization shots. Every human has a different tolerance to different things. For example, one of my kids can drink as much caffeine as he wants, and it doesn't affect his behavior. At the same time, I can't let one of my other children have caffeine. In my earlier years on the party scene, I had some friends who could drink until they passed out without any effect on their behavior. I've seen others drink one beer, get wild, and want to fight. It makes no sense to me at all how the medical field can justify giving all children the exact same shots on the exact schedule when every human on earth has a completely different DNA. I've even heard a presidential candidate make the same statement that I've been making for years about vaccinations. I'm not in any way putting down the medical field, because I believe with all my heart they are needed and that they are doing their very best to help people. It is a fact that autism is an epidemic all over the world that continues to bring hardships on families by the way of financial ruin and strained relationships. It is my opinion that it would be helpful if the medical field teamed up with the natural doctors.

Personally, I have learned more about life through autism than all my other life experiences combined. I now understand more clearly how God loves his children. I have also learned that the most important things in life aren't things. Lastly, I have learned that what the devil intended for bad, God turned it into a blessing.

Word of Advice

Dads, don't waste time arguing with folks over the cause of autism. Encourage your wife to stay out of that losing battle too! Trust me, it will only result in hurt feelings, and it will absolutely accomplish zero. Focus your time on your family and the treatments that work for your autistic child. I only included the previous chapter in hopes that our experience provides help for the cure.

Chapter 17

OLD SCHOOL BUSINESS

Autism forced me to go into business for myself, and I have learned more about the economy and how to fix it than all my college years and past employment combined. Small business is the backbone of the country's economy and is overlooked, to say the least. Small business is the number one creator of jobs in the U.S. Most small business folks remember where they come from and will treat you better than big companies. The economy is simple. We need to make our own products and trade with our friends. There is absolutely no reason why every able bodied person in America should not have a job. Small business owners truly live in the real world and for the most part will go out of their way to help their fellow man.

I grew up old school with older parents and grandparents, and I miss the simple life. In my lifetime, a lot of mom and pop stores have shut down due to the competition of big business and it seems that it gets harder every year for them to keep the doors open. In the past five years, I've worked for hundreds of small businesses but only a handful of big businesses, and the big businesses usually make me wait thirty to sixty days to collect my money.

I've learned that success can't be measured entirely by dollars and cents. In fact, I put my favorite scripture for success on my GOD BLESS THE LITTLE MAN TRUCK windshield where I could look at it every time I drive it. "By humility and fear of the Lord are riches, honor and life" (Proverbs 22-4). That is God's definition of success and anything less than that is a successful failure.

I grew up in a time where a handshake was better than a legal document. My Dad always told me that it was better to know that you could go borrow a hundred thousand dollars and be broke than to have a hundred thousand dollars and no credit. Successful small business understands this. As a small business owner, I know that it is detrimental to the well-being of my family to lose my good name. Word of mouth is the best advertisement! If you want to be successful, you need to be friendly and provide great service to your customers. As a result, they will tell their friends about you. I try to spend my money with my friends; they are depending on sales to feed their families.

Chapter 18

GOD'S PURPOSE FOR ME

As I mentioned earlier, I surrendered to God to do whatever He wanted me to do with the hopes that He wouldn't send me to a foreign mission field. After much prayer and soul searching, it is clear that God wants me to use my talents to help others and make this a better place to live and do business. The only two real talents I have are motivation and the ability to make people laugh, so that's the card I intend to play. It is simple. Spread the gospel, show others how to be successful, and give them a good clean laugh to go with it.

Melina and I started a ministry called GOD BLESS THE LITTLE MAN. This name fit autistic children as well as the small business owners everywhere. Our website is www.godblessthelittleman.com. Feel free to check it out and see what we are all about. We want to educate the public on autism awareness and encourage families to stay together.

Also, I plan to do motivational speeches directed toward spreading the gospel, autism awareness, small business promotion, and drug abuse prevention.

This book is mainly focused on fathers, but I hope that it brings much encouragement to anyone dealing with a special needs child. God bless you and please feel free to post a comment or ask a question on our website godblessthelittleman.com. "Be of good courage and He will strengthen your heart, all ye that hope in the Lord" (Psalms 31:24).

As Christians, we all have a purpose in this life. I don't consider myself to be an evangelist or a traditional preacher. I'm a hillbilly with a formal education! Also, I have a wide array of white and blue collared work experience. Dads, use your God given talents to make a difference in this world and encourage others to do the same!

24 Faith Based Tips for Daily Living

Tip 1

ACCEPTANCE

This is the most important tip because you have to get past it for the others to work. My mom gave me this piece of advice growing up and in fact preached it to all of her children. She said that no matter what you were dealing with, the hardest part is accepting it. She was so right because a person will stay in a constant mental fight until he has accepted his situation. The word of God teaches that "a double minded man is unstable in all his ways" (James 1:8). Fathers, don't live in denial. If you have an autistic child, face up to it and look your problems in the eyes.

Tip 2

MINDSET

Nothing in life comes our way without first crossing God's desk. He knows the big picture, and we have to trust him with our situations no matter how challenging they are at the time. From my experience, He allows us to go through tough times to build our faith and prepare us for something bigger. Trust me dads, if you will cast your cares upon the one that cares for you and have a prayerful attitude, He will give you the strength to walk through the valley with peace and joy. The Bible also says, "As a man thinks that's what he is" (Proverbs 23:7). Think of yourself as a winner through Christ Jesus. Hold your head high and refuse to think on the negatives. March forward with hope each day. God has made you the CEO of your joy, and nothing can touch it without your consent. Think like a winner, dress like a winner, walk like a winner, conduct business like a winner, and most importantly, be a Christian and family man.

Tip 3

PLANNING

Some of my most unsuccessful and depressing days are usually a bi-product of poor planning. While it is impossible to map out your entire future, you do have to have some kind of idea which direction you are headed. In my senior year of college, I had a business marketing class that was ninety percent focused on time management and the proper way to effectively use a day planner. I can honestly say this class helped me to take success to a new found level. For example, if I only completed seven tasks on list for the day, it wasn't because I forgot to do the other three. I simply prioritized my schedule and made a conscious decision to bump the not so squeaky wheels to the next day. The Bible says, "For which of you, intending to build a tower, does not sit down first and count the cost, whether he has enough to finish it" (Luke 14:28). Put a plan of action together with realistic goals and work diligently toward the future without missing the blessings each new day brings. Also, the past is only good for drawing wisdom and strength, so do not camp out there. Dads, you desperately have to get the most out of each day when raising a special needs child. An hour saved each day is priceless to you and the rest of your family.

Tip 4

JOURNALING

Dads, purchase a cheap daily journal and use it every day. If you are a morning person, write in it for five to ten minutes while you are drinking coffee. If you are a night owl like me, write in it after the kids go to bed. Log your feelings, worries, and events that transpired that day. Chart the goals for the future days and weeks to come. Other than the word of God, this tool has helped me more than anything, and I still use it today. Journaling relieves stress and makes for great therapy. Make sure that you put all the good things down too because this gives you a sense of accomplishment. A journal will give you a daily reality check and sound proof way of tracking your success as the months go by. I'm always amazed at how things that worried me in past days were a complete waste of my time and how most things work themselves out.

Tip 5

TAPPING OUT

On the very dark days when it seems there is no way out and no hope in sight and the world you live in has become a place of uttermost despair, play this card. Go to a very quiet place and kick back. Shut your eyes and set a one to two hour time limit. A wooded area or a body of water has always been my choice of a get-a-way. I personally would use two hours most times because it would take that long to get my head out of the sand. I would tell myself that I'm giving up for the allotted time and have absolutely zero responsibilities to anyone or anything and can in no way go on. Then I would pray to God and tell him that there is no way I can make it another day if he didn't show up. My next prayer would be Lord please help me to have the desire to even want to help myself. Believe it or not, my best days would usually follow. It's amazing how letting it all go for a couple of hours will let the stress completely go. I know this one sounds crazy, but it works. Desperate times call for desperate measures! Jesus was perfect, and he had to get away from the noise of the crowd. He headed to the hills from time to time, so don't put yourself above Him. The toughest MMA fighter will TAP OUT when he has had all he can take.

Tip 6

COUNT YOUR BLESSINGS

Take inventory of all the things in your life that money can't buy such as salvation, family, true friends, and health. Focus on the simple things like mobility, food, clothing, shelter, and God given talent. Spend your time praying for people who are in worse shape than you instead of using it to feel sorry for yourself. Take the time to write it down, and you can see that the good in your life strongly out- weighs the bad.

Tip 7

BE DIFFERENT

Again, Jesus left us a perfect example to follow. His whole life was about being different. He was King of Kings and Lord of Lords, but He was born in a stable. He built his ministry traveling with a rough bunch of folks. He loved his enemies, even the ones who rejected him. He also showed mercy to the vilest of sinners. Choose to be different than everyone else in everything you do. Variety is the spice of life, so make it interesting. Relocate, change career paths, mow your yard backwards, drive a different way home from work, try a new restaurant, join a gym, or take your wife to a surprise get-a-way. By all means, don't get stuck in the same old dull routine. The word of God says we are to be a "peculiar people" (1 Peter 2:9), plus it will keep your neighbors wondering what crazy move comes next.

Tip 8

FAKE IT UNTIL YOU MAKE IT

When all else fails, fake it until you make it. Personally, I have never liked being around fake people, but this is different. Fake people are simply trying to impress others by acting or pretending they are something different than what they really are for selfish reasons. Actually, faking for therapy is you trying to make yourself feel good about yourself until it becomes natural. You are actually trying to fool yourself rather than the general public. Put a smile on, and sooner or later, it will come natural! Use positive words and say positive things in every area of conversation. Surround yourself with positive people. I once heard it said “People are like elevators. They either bring you up or take you down.” From my life experiences, they were spot on.

Tip 9

INNER STRENGTH

For the believer, the word of God promises us that "He that is in us is greater than He that is in the world" (1 John 4:4). The Bible also says, "For we wrestle not against flesh and blood, but against principalities, against powers, against the rulers of the darkness of this world, against spiritual wickedness in high places" (Ephesians 6:12). Focus on the inner man and always remember that this life is temporary. We are therefore eternal beings. If we only had a glimpse of Heaven, we would be willing to stand on our heads if need be until we got there. No person or situation can intimidate you without your consent, and no person or situation can make you mad. Whether you know it or not, you have to actually make a decision to be mad. Exercise discipline and self-control on a daily basis because you will need it to face the challenges of autism.

Tip 10

HELP SOMEONE

Do something to help your fellow man. It always blesses me to help someone else, plus it is a great way to get my mind off my problems. I've found that there are always plenty of unfortunate people out there who have worse problems than I do. You have to be careful with this one because some people will take advantage of your good nature. You can help people that are truly trying to help themselves. My Dad has told me on more than one occasion that not everyone that has his hand up wants help. He may just want to pull you down with him. Also, it is a waste of time to try to help self-righteous arrogant people too. This one has caused me a great deal of disappointment. A humble person will show you a multitude of gratitude when you offer your time to give him a hand or show him a better way to do something.

Tip 11

NEVER GIVE UP

Giving up is not an option. You can TAP OUT for a one to two hour therapy session, but that's it. The word of God says that "weeping may endure for the night but joy comes in the morning" (Psalm 30:5). It also says "His mercies are new every day" (Lamentations 3:22-23). Remember the old saying momma said there would be days like this? Face the fact that you are simply going to have a bad day from time to time. Things are not going to go your way or the way you intended, but hang on a day or two and try to have a good attitude. It will eventually get better. Anyone can quit or live a defeated life, but it takes courage to press on with a smile on your face when the chips are down. My Dad has often told me a hero only dies once, but a coward dies a thousand deaths. Choose to be a winner today!

Tip 12

PROMISE BOOK

Buy a Bible scripture promise book and keep it with you wherever you go. Believe, accept, and cling to God's promises as they apply to your life. Memorize as many scriptures as you can and hide them in your heart. The book I personally use has one thousand promises and it is a must have for me. These books cost one dollar each if you buy at least a hundred. You might consult with your pastor and stock up for the entire church.

Tip 13

SPIRIT MAN

Read the word of God and find as much Christian material from reputable authors as you can find on the areas of life that challenge you. Build your faith muscles and put the whole armor of God on every day as you face life. "Be sober, be vigilant; because your adversary the devil, as a roaring lion, walketh about, seeking whom he may devour" (1 Peter 5:8) He would like nothing better than to destroy your marriage and your life. An old Indian chief once compared the spirit man and the flesh man as a white dog and a black dog fighting. When asked which one was going to win, he said the one that you feed the most.

Tip 14

SCHEDULE

Maintain a well- organized day planner and keep a good daily, weekly, and monthly schedule. This tool will keep your mind sharp and keep you from wasting time. It will also allow you to get the most of each day. In raising an autistic child, it takes a very strict schedule to fit everything into your life. Doctor appointments, therapy sessions, meal planning, and carving time out to make a living and meet all of your other obligations will overwhelm you if you try to fly by the seat of your pants.

Tip 15

BE PROACTIVE

Take charge of your situation. Study the habits of your autistic child to familiarize yourself with what makes him or her tick and be ready to address it. Do not by any means live reactively to your situation, or you will stay in a constant fog trying to maintain sanity. Do what works best for your family and give no thought to what others may think or do. They are not in your situation and have no way of really knowing what they would do or how they would deal with life if they had your shoes on for one day. If I had a dollar for every time a well-meaning person stared at us or told us how he could straighten Luke out if he had him at his house, I would be a very wealthy man. Again, the purpose of this book is to share what worked for me in hopes that God allows it to find you and help you push on with peace and joy.

Tip 16

PATIENCE

The word of God says that tribulations worketh patience (Romans 5:3). I must say, I have paid a great deal of life lesson tuition for this one. The best way to pray is "Lord, please help me to have patience from my past experiences." Study the most patient person you know and try to learn from him. Be slow to speak, quick to listen, and slow to anger. While raising Luke, I became a person I did not like. I was easily offended, full of bitterness, and quick to go head to head and let someone have it if he so much as looked at us wrong. Don't get too up or too down in your emotions or you will make a regretful jumpy move. Calmly let them know with a loving heart that your child is autistic when they stare at you or make rude comments. Think about how you would have looked at someone else's child before you had an autistic child and the knowledge of this most challenging disorder.

Tip 17

GOD'S EYES

Look at your child through God's eyes. Your child may be a challenge, but he or she is a blessing from God. God does not make mistakes, and he does not break promises. Ten years with Luke has been a rough road, but I would not be the man I am today had I not experienced autism first hand. I also know that Luke brings me a joy that is different than my other four children, and I couldn't imagine life without him. God sees the whole picture and knows us better than we know ourselves!

Tip 18

DO NOT FRET

Don't give way to the fear of what your child will be like or what's going to happen in the future. This is a complete waste of time and energy, not to mention there is nothing you can do about it today. The word of God says, "He has not given us the spirit of fear; but of power, and of love, and of a sound mind" (II Timothy 1:7). The Bible also says, "Do not worry about tomorrow, for tomorrow will worry about its own things. Sufficient for the day is its own trouble" (Mathew 6:11). Rest and trust in God's love, and He will make a way for you and your family. He is with us in this life and has promised an eternal life to all believers. Living in constant fear will cause you to make bad decisions, have poor job performance, and have an unhealthy personal and family life. Surrender all your fears to God and trust Him to take care of all the what-ifs.

Tip 19

PHYSICAL WELL BEING

Dads, take good care of your health. Get plenty of sleep and exercise. Also, carve out a little leisure time for yourself. Just because you have an autistic child doesn't mean you can't have a life. As I mentioned earlier, "The devil is like a roaring lion seeking whom he may devour" (1 Peter 5:8). If you have ever watched wild animals on a nature show, you would agree that the lion always goes for the weak first. To face the challenges of autism, you need to stay strong spiritually, mentally, and physically. Also, physical exercise makes for a great stress reliever.

Tip 20

MOMMA

Take good care of Momma. This is very important men! If you are like me, you get so focused on trying to make the living and do all the chores of life while dealing with the challenges of autism, you completely forget about your wife. Don't forget she was once that pretty young lady you were so excited to hang out with. Get a babysitter and take her out on the town. If you are like us and it's near impossible to find someone to watch the kids, get them to bed early and have a movie night. Dress up like you plan to go to a five star restaurant and really talk to her and make her feel special. Pretend you guys are dating. By all means, don't talk about the kids or any of the major issues of life or it will not have the same effect.

Tip 21

EMBRACE

Embrace your situation. Don't be bitter, embarrassed, or feel awkward. Don't look at other people and feel like your family is missing out on the good life. The fact is your life may be better than theirs. You can't always judge a book by its cover. Also, it is very easy to become jealous of people that don't have your specific challenge. Don't allow yourself or your family to play the victim card. Trust me; you don't have a bad life. It is just a different life. The word of God says, "A sound heart is the life of the flesh: but envy the rottenness of bones" (Proverbs 14:30). It also says, "Come unto me all ye that labor and are heavy laden, and I will give you rest" (Matthew 11:28).

Tip 22

STAYING SOCIALLY ACTIVE

Don't become a prisoner in your home like we did for years. Be as normal as the next family and by all means stay busy. I've always heard an idle mind is the Devil's workshop, and there's a lot of truth to that. Always be reaching for something and stay excited about the next step in life. Press forward to the high calling of Christ Jesus and refuse to live a defeated life. Anyone can dig a hole and hide. Choose to get the best out of each day no matter what it throws at you! Refuse to let the challenges of autism keep you from receiving God's best for your family. Invite friends to your house on a regular basis and find a loving church that understands your situation. In our experience, we found that smaller churches worked better for us. The bigger churches and the crowds seemed to overstimulate Luke and make him uncomfortable.

Tip 23

HUMILITY AND CONTENTMENT

The Bible says that by "humility and fear of the Lord are riches, honor, and life" (Proverbs 22:4). You can have a lot of money and be what I call a successful failure. Stay humble, be content, work hard, laugh often, show love for your fellow man, give God the credit, and get ready to enjoy life despite its challenges. The word of God says, "That whosoever therefore shall humble himself as this little child, the same is the greatest in the kingdom of heaven" (Matthew 18:4). It also says, "It is better to be of a humble spirit with the lowly, than to divide the spoil with the proud" (Proverbs 16:19) Be content in all the areas of your life, and it will bring you an abundance of satisfaction.

Tip 24

LAUGHTER

This is the best medicine that isn't available on the shelf. Growing up in a family of eight with little money produced some comedians at the Gowen house. We were always trying to one-up each other. My Dad is seventy nine, and he is still the master smart aleck. He is a sixteen year old boy inside an old body. In fact, he told me he never felt old until a few years ago when he was visiting the nursing home. He said as he was leaving, several of the nurses and orderlies stared at him as if one of the residents was making a break for it. The Bible teaches that "a merry heart doeth good like a medicine: but a broken spirit drieth the bones" (Proverbs 17:22). This is so true. I've always heard that misery enjoys company, but that is not all together true. It enjoys the same kind of company. The golden rule for laughter is to laugh with someone and not at them. Furthermore, whatever you laugh at has to be funny to all people and not be offensive. A smile is the universal language among all humans, and more times than not you will get one in return. With the rising cost of living, and the financial strain that many Americans are facing each day, who wouldn't want something for free? It is a true gift if you can get someone to smile or laugh to relieve the pressures of life temporarily!

About the Author

Charles J. Gowen is a Christian husband and father of five. In an effort to meet the needs of his autistic son Luke, he left the corporate world and started a tree service five years ago. He wrote this book to help other fathers deal with the hardships and challenges of autism. God has truly restored joy to Jerry's entire family and he is excited to tell his story!